# Roseanne Arnold

THE ACHIEVERS

# Roseanne Arnold

## COMEDY'S QUEEN BEE

### Katherine E. Krohn

 Lerner Publications Company ▪ Minneapolis

*For Sarah Dvorah,*
*with special thanks to Phelps*

*This book is available in two bindings:*
Library binding by Lerner Publications Company
Soft cover by First Avenue Editions
241 First Avenue North
Minneapolis, MN 55401


LIBRARY OF CONGRESS CATALOGING-IN-PUBLICATION DATA

**Krohn, Katherine E.**
   Roseanne Arnold : comedy's queen bee / Katherine E. Krohn.
      p.   cm. — (The Achievers)
   Summary: Examines the life and career of the successful
comedian and television star, covering her childhood, family,
stand-up comedy act, and acting projects.
   ISBN 0-8225-0520-7 (library binding)
   ISBN 0-8225-9644-X (paperback)
   1. Arnold, Roseanne—Juvenile literature.  2. Comedians—
United States—Biography—Juvenile literature.  3. Television
actors and actresses—United States—Biography—Juvenile
literature. [1. Arnold, Roseanne. 2. Comedians. 3. Actors and
actresses.] I. Title.  II. Series.
PN2287.B23K76   1993
792.7'028'092—dc20
[B]
                                                    92-42653
                                                       CIP
                                                        AC

1   2   3   4   5   6   98   97   96   95   94   93

# Contents

The Conners: Roseanne, Darlene, Becky, D.J., and Dan

# 1
## Show Time

Roseanne Conner has just been laid off from her job on the assembly line at Wellman Plastics. Her husband, Dan, just lost a big construction job that he was banking on. Who is going to feed their three kids? Who will pay the mortgage on their house?

Desperate, Roseanne takes the only job she can find: a fast-food position at Chicken Divine. At the new job, Roseanne must take orders from a teenage boss—20 years younger than she is. "Your life doesn't always turn out the way you planned it," she remarks. "Sometimes you have to do things you never thought you would do in a million years."

No one knows better how plans can go wrong than Roseanne Arnold, star of America's highest-rated TV comedy, *Roseanne*. While she is now one of the most powerful and wealthy women in Hollywood, Arnold never loses sight of the difficult years she experienced before she found fame.

As Roseanne Conner, the character she created for television, Roseanne Arnold pays tribute to people who work hard and struggle to make ends meet. Unlike many TV families, the Conners are not rich, beautiful, or famous. They live in a cluttered, two-story house in the working-class town of Lanford, Illinois. They fight, complain about school, and worry about money—just like ordinary people.

Since the show first aired, Roseanne Conner has held many low-paying jobs. She's been a factory worker, a fast-food server, and a waitress. She's sold products over the telephone. Although Roseanne is barely able to pay the bills, she refuses to view herself as a victim.

Roseanne Conner, her sister Jackie (left), and her friend Crystal (right) take a break from their jobs on the assembly line.

Roseanne also refuses to be silent about the injustice she sees around her. She fights for workers' rights at Wellman Plastics, and she declares "discrimination" when she discovers that the job of Mrs. Claus at the local department store pays less than the job of Santa.

*Roseanne* doesn't hesitate to face tough issues head on. In a straightforward and often funny way, Roseanne Conner and her two teenage daughters discuss birth control, sex, and dating. Roseanne and her sister talk about child abuse, women's rights, and aging. Viewers—young people and parents alike—can learn a lot about frank communication from the Conner family.

*Roseanne* first aired on ABC-TV in October 1988. The show was an instant success and has consistently topped television's Nielsen ratings. More than 31.7 million people watch *Roseanne* each week. In August 1992, more viewers tuned in for a Tuesday night *Roseanne* rerun than watched the Republican National Convention broadcast on the same evening.

Why do Roseanne Arnold's fans like her so much? Because she's not just funny, she's also *genuine*. "I play a real mom on my show," Arnold explains. "She doesn't clean her house. She isn't sweet all the time. And she doesn't pay attention to her kids and husband."

In one episode, Roseanne waits until her children have left for school before shuffling into the kitchen in her robe and slippers. "I love 'em and everything," she tells her husband, "I just ain't in the mood."

Roseanne Conner's sarcasm and sloppy language delight some viewers and offend others. "Yeah, she's crude," writes critic Barbara Ehrenreich in the *New Republic*, "but so are the realities of pain and exploitation she seeks to remind us of."

A talented team of actors makes up the *Roseanne* cast. John Goodman portrays Roseanne's big-hearted husband, Dan, and Laurie Metcalf plays Jackie, Roseanne's free-thinking and energetic younger sister.

Arnold personally interviewed and selected the actors who would play her on-screen children. She chose Lecy Goranson to depict the boy-crazy teenage daughter, Becky. Sara Gilbert won the part of Darlene, the moody and sarcastic middle child. Michael Fishman was chosen to play Roseanne and Dan's young son, D.J.

Several well-known performers have also been featured in *Roseanne*'s supporting cast. Comedian-actor Martin Mull portrayed Roseanne's uptight boss at Rodbell's Coffee Shop, and he recently joined *Roseanne*'s 16-member writing crew. In 1991 comic Tom Arnold (Roseanne's real-life husband) came on board as Dan's dopey high school buddy, Arnie. Outrageous comedian Sandra Bernhard plays Nancy, Jackie's good friend and Arnie's ex-wife. Veteran film actress Estelle Parsons plays Roseanne's overbearing mother.

*Roseanne* has been television's top-rated comedy series for several seasons. Yet the show itself has never even been *nominated* for an Emmy award. Year after year, the Academy of Television Arts and Sciences has shut *Roseanne* out of its competition. At the 1992 awards show, several cast members, including Roseanne Arnold, were nominated for Emmys. Just one cast member, supporting actress Laurie Metcalf, won a trophy.

Why has the Hollywood establishment refused to give the number-one comedy show the top honor in television? Could it be that Roseanne Arnold's commitment to truth and honesty has made people uncomfortable?

Roseanne's TV family takes after her real family.

Roseanne and Tom Arnold are inseparable.

Roseanne thinks that Hollywood is simply out of touch with ordinary working people. "They don't get what the most-watched show is about," she explains. "They have that snobbish thing about shows about blue-collar people."

Even without Emmy awards, Roseanne Arnold remains popular with those who mean the most to her— her fans. She has captured numerous People's Choice and Golden Globe awards, and she's earned a celebrity star on Hollywood's Walk of Fame.

Roseanne will continue to express herself through an innovative TV show that springs straight from her heart. "I think about the people out there," she says. "They're awesome fans. Plus, I think they are so much like me."

# 2
## Funny Girl

"Comedian! Comedian!"

Roseanne Barr dashed to the television set. "Comedian!" her father shouted, turning up the volume on *The Ed Sullivan Show*. As always, when there was a funny person on TV, Jerry Barr called his daughter Roseanne to watch.

Her eyes sparkling, Roseanne fixed her attention on Bob Hope, Milton Berle, or another popular comedian of the 1950s. She would laugh aloud and remember his jokes. Later, she would tell the jokes to her friends and family. "We could say anything we wanted to in my home," Roseanne recalls, "as long as it was funny."

Roseanne Barr was born on November 3, 1952, in Salt Lake City, Utah. Roseanne's father, Jerry, was a door-to-door salesperson. For a while he sold blankets and later, patio furniture. Roseanne's mother, Helen, worked as a homemaker.

Roseanne had two younger sisters, Geraldine and Stephanie, and a younger brother, Ben. While the Barr family was Jewish, most other people living in Salt Lake City were Mormons. The Barrs felt pressure to fit in with their neighbors. They attended a Jewish synagogue on Saturdays and a Mormon church on Sundays. "It was very painful to be different," Roseanne remembers.

Roseanne and her sisters and brother liked to spend time with their grandmother, Bobbe Mary (*bobbe* is the Yiddish word for grandmother). Bobbe Mary, or "Bubs," owned and managed an old apartment house on Park Street in Salt Lake City. For a while, Roseanne and her family lived in Bubs's building.

Roseanne would climb the stairs to Bubs's apartment, bang on the screen door "in just the right spot," and the door would swing open. "What do you want to eat?" Bubs would always ask.

"I loved my grandmother more than any other human being," Roseanne says, "because she never lied, never told you what you wanted to hear, never compromised."

When Roseanne was just a toddler, her parents hired a teenage girl named Robbie to help take care of her. Robbie was a tall, good-natured girl from Tennessee. She wore baggy overalls, chewed tobacco, and called Roseanne "Lil Bit." Robbie played Elvis Presley records and showed young Roseanne how to dance.

Roseanne's hometown—Salt Lake City, Utah

Roseanne liked dancing, and she begged her parents to let her take tap dance lessons. Roseanne loved to perform. She wrote poetry, stories, and plays. She and the neighborhood kids would perform her plays in the backyard. The shows typically starred Roseanne and ended with her saving the world.

Roseanne had a secret childhood wish. "One day I would be a gypsy," she dreamed, "and be able to take a knapsack and travel all over the world, having incredible adventures, making campfires, and cooking beans in cans."

When Roseanne was 16, she had a serious accident. She was hit by a car and flipped high into the air.

15

At East High School, Rose-anne liked to crack jokes. But she was not always happy as a teenager.

When she landed, the car's hood ornament smashed into her head. Roseanne was rushed to a hospital by ambulance.

She was semiconscious for days, and the doctors believed she might die. Eventually, Roseanne recovered, leaving the doctors and her family relieved and amazed.

Before long Roseanne went into a hospital again — but this time for a very different reason. When Roseanne was 17, her parents admitted her to a mental health ward at the Utah State Hospital. Roseanne was an unhappy teenager, and she frequently fought with her parents. Jerry and Helen Barr thought their daughter needed psychological treatment.

Roseanne didn't like the hospital. "It was a horrifying place," she remembers. But she had been unhappy living at home, too. Roseanne stayed in the hospital for more than eight months. Then she moved back home and planned for her future—which did not include returning to her school, Salt Lake City's East High.

Roseanne didn't plan on getting pregnant, either—but she did. Mr. and Mrs. Barr, upset and embarrassed by the pregnancy, offered their daughter little support. Unmarried, 18 years old, and desperate, Roseanne moved to Denver, Colorado.

"I got on welfare and rented a room for 50 bucks a month," she recalls. "I turned on the water and cockroaches came out of the spigot."

Roseanne knew she needed help. She moved into a Salvation Army home for teenage mothers. There, Roseanne's first child, a girl, was born on May 16, 1971. Within a few weeks, Roseanne made a difficult decision. Because she felt she wasn't financially or emotionally prepared to care for a child, she gave her baby up for adoption.

Jewish Family and Children's Services in Denver found a home for Roseanne's baby. On the day the social workers came to take her daughter, Roseanne whispered to the baby, "You remember this—I'll see you when you're 18." Roseanne was certain that one day she would be reunited with her daughter.

Roseanne packed up her belongings and went to live with a former schoolmate, Linda Rizzardi, in Georgetown, Colorado. Georgetown was an artists' community sitting high in the Rocky Mountains, 60 miles west of Denver.

Roseanne liked Georgetown instantly—especially the fresh mountain air and the friendly people. Within a few days, she landed a job bussing tables at the Silver Queen, a French restaurant.

Before long Linda introduced Roseanne to a man named Bill Pentland, who worked as a night clerk at the Motor Inn motel. "He was really weird," Roseanne remembers. "I loved him right away." Roseanne and Bill dated for a couple of years and were married on February 4, 1973.

Roseanne and Bill moved into a small mobile home in Denver. In three years they had three babies— Jessica, Jennifer, and Jake. Bill found work as a garbage truck driver and then as a postal clerk. For a few years, Roseanne worked as a full-time mom. "We never had any money," she remembers. "I made all my kids' clothes out of pillowcases."

Though she was poor and had a hard time making ends meet, Roseanne's home life was happy. "I'd wait for Bill to come home at 4:30, serve Hamburger Helper and Jell-O and a salad, and we'd sit for hours passionately discussing music, art, and philosophy," Roseanne wrote in her 1989 autobiography, *Roseanne: My Life as a Woman.*

In the early 1980s, Roseanne discovered the Denver writers' community. Every week, she and her sister Geraldine—who had also moved to Denver—would meet with a group of writers at the Woman to Woman Bookstore on Colfax Street. The women would sit around on musty old furniture and drink tea. They would tell stories, read essays and poetry aloud, and discuss books they had read.

Roseanne wrote about being a wife and mother—the subjects she knew best. She transformed the ordinary events of her life into funny and insightful stories. The other women laughed at her jokes and appreciated her point of view.

Roseanne volunteered at the bookstore for a short time. But money was tight at home, and she soon had to look for a paying position. In 1981 Roseanne took a job as a cocktail waitress at a Denver restaurant and soon put her unique sense of humor to work. While delivering food and drinks, Roseanne also delivered jokes. "The drinks are six bucks," she would say to the customers, "but it'll cost you three dollars more for me to take them off the tray."

Customers liked Roseanne—she made them laugh. They came back to the restaurant again and again just to hear her wisecracks. One day one of Roseanne's regular customers suggested that she audition at Comedy Works, a local comedy club.

Roseanne hesitated—but not for long. She knew she liked to perform and to make people laugh. Why not? She would give it a try!

"America: Here I Come."

# 3
# *Domestic Goddess*

Roseanne's nervousness barely showed as she stood on the Comedy Works stage and munched Chee-tos from a bag. "The day I care about cleaning my house," Roseanne matter-of-factly announced, "is the day Sears comes out with a riding vacuum cleaner."

The Audition Night audience laughed and cheered. Never before had they seen a comedian like Roseanne Barr. The women in the audience appreciated Roseanne's honesty. She could take an ordinary domestic situation, the kind many people share, and turn it into something funny. Men liked Roseanne too—she made them laugh at themselves.

Roseanne was a heavy woman. So she included jokes about dieting, food, and exercise in her routine. "Do you want my recipe for trailmix?" she asked. "Plain M&Ms, Kraft Caramels, and Peanut M&Ms. Gets me over those mountains!"

The audience roared. When Roseanne walked off-stage after her audition, many people, including the club's owner, were convinced that Roseanne Barr was an important new stand-up comic. The manager of Comedy Works offered Roseanne a weekly spot at the club. She soon had a following—regular fans who came to every one of her performances.

Roseanne wanted to keep her act fresh, so she worked hard to develop new material. With her sister Geraldine's help, she created an innovative comedy act—the Domestic Goddess routine—that would sky-rocket her to the heights of fame.

Eagerly, Roseanne tried out her new act at Comedy Works: "I never get out of the house," she whined. "I never have any fun—ever, ever, ever—because I'm a housewife. I hate that word—I want to be called 'Domestic Goddess.'"

The crowd loved the new act. Soon, Roseanne's sidesplitting Domestic Goddess routine was a favorite at clubs all over Denver.

For two years, Roseanne worked part-time as a comic and part-time as a homemaker. Although Bill Pentland encouraged Roseanne's talents, he saw his wife's interest in comedy as just a hobby. Roseanne had other ideas. She wanted a career in show business.

In 1983 Roseanne's friends encouraged her to audition at the Comedy Store, a well-known club in Los Angeles, California. A lot of famous comedians, including Robin Williams, Sandra Bernhard, Paula Poundstone, and Richard Pryor, launched their careers at the Comedy Store. The club's owner, Mitzi Shore, especially encouraged female comics.

Roseanne didn't know if her routine would be appreciated in Los Angeles. She knew the trip to California was a gamble. But she was also at a crucial point in her career—she had to move ahead.

Roseanne would try her luck in Los Angeles, among Hollywood's biggest comics.

Roseanne and her first husband, Bill Pentland

Bill stayed behind with the kids, while Roseanne and Geraldine headed to L.A. They checked into the Hilton Hotel and immediately called the Comedy Store to arrange an audition. The manager scheduled Roseanne to perform the next evening in the club's audition room, a small stage where unknown performers tried out their material.

To celebrate the upcoming audition, Roseanne and Geraldine went out to an expensive Hollywood restaurant. They drank champagne and ate caviar. They both felt that something important and wonderful was about to happen.

Roseanne and Geraldine were right. "The night I auditioned for Mitzi Shore," Roseanne remembers, "I went on the stage for six minutes and blew the room away."

Shore was so impressed that she did something unusual. Immediately following the audition, she moved Roseanne from the small audition stage to the club's main room. There, Roseanne took her place among the club's big-name comics.

Roseanne performed nightly at the Comedy Store. Within a week, she was "discovered." Jim McCawley, a talent scout from *The Tonight Show*, approached Roseanne after her act one evening. He invited her to appear on the popular television variety show—in two days!

So excited her knees were shaking, Roseanne gave the talent scout a "yes" and hurried out of the club. Geraldine followed closely behind. On the way back to the hotel, Roseanne told her sister the news. They hugged, jumped up and down, and danced with joy in the hotel parking lot for an hour.

Two days later, Roseanne performed her Domestic Goddess routine on national television. The audience roared, as did *Tonight Show* host Johnny Carson.

Backstage, a talent agent named Herb Nanas watched Roseanne on a monitor. "Does she have a manager?" he asked Jim McCawley. "I want to meet her. I'm going to make her the biggest star in America."

When she came backstage after her performance, Roseanne met with Nanas. He told her that he wanted every housewife in the country to say: "I'm a Domestic Goddess!"

Roseanne looked at Nanas in astonishment. Close to tears, she replied: "Everything I ever dreamed would happen in my lifetime, you just said to me in the last five minutes."

Nanas was quick to put Roseanne to work. He booked her on a tour with Louie Anderson, another heavyset comic. The tour, called "Wait 'Til We Eat," visited cities all over the United States. The act had a food theme; invitations to the show were shaped like spatulas. In Las Vegas, Roseanne and Louie held a press conference in the kitchen of Caesar's Palace nightclub.

Roseanne made more TV appearances and performed solo in clubs across the country. She was a guest on *Late Night with David Letterman*, and she returned to *The Tonight Show* several times.

Roseanne felt powerful on stage, and her confidence showed. "When I'm on stage, nobody is funnier or better than me," she said. Roseanne's jokes weren't always upbeat and lighthearted though. She sometimes explored the dark side of relationships, marriage, families, and everyday life. Many of Roseanne's jokes were based on pain, anger, and her own personal problems.

Roseanne's humor made some people uncomfortable.

Men sometimes became upset when Roseanne encouraged women not to be victims. "I...tell [women] to turn the fear around," she said. "Be as threatening, big, looming, loudmouthed, and unfeminine as you can possibly dig down in your gut to be."

Hollywood had a narrow view of how a female performer should look and behave. Roseanne didn't fit the mold. She was neither thin nor sweet-natured. Some people made fun of Roseanne's weight. Others criticized her for being blunt and outspoken.

Roseanne and Bill share a laugh with Louie Anderson.

Roseanne cuts loose on *The Roseanne Barr Show.*

Roseanne ignored the critics. She was not about to change her style or compromise her beliefs because of a few bad reviews. Besides, most people loved Roseanne's loud, boisterous humor. She was gaining a nationwide following.

In 1986, Herb Nanas arranged for Roseanne to star in a Home Box Office (HBO) cable television special, *The Roseanne Barr Show.* Roseanne was also the show's principal scriptwriter.

The special featured Roseanne as a gum-chewing

stand-up comic. She performed on a stage that looked like an ordinary living room. At different points in her routine, Roseanne walked offstage, onto another set—a trailer modelled after her real home.

There, Roseanne performed madcap skits with a family that closely resembled her own. Child actors played Roseanne's children, while comedian Tom Arnold stood in as Roseanne's husband. Even Geraldine had a part in the show: she played a mad scientist in a fake TV commercial.

When she finished taping the HBO special, Roseanne was certain she wanted to continue performing on television. She was tired of touring the country, and she missed being at home with her husband and children. She called Nanas and told him she wanted her own television show.

Many producers were interested in working with Roseanne. She received a variety of offers and read several scripts, but none of them seemed right. She was offered supporting roles in two popular situation comedies. Roseanne stubbornly refused these parts, insisting that she wanted her *own* show.

Finally, the right offer came through. Tom Werner and Marcy Carsey, who produced the award-winning *Cosby Show*, approached Roseanne with an idea. They wanted to create a situation comedy about a working-class family who had real problems and an undefeatable sense of humor. Roseanne loved the idea.

Werner and Carsey were excited to work with Roseanne. They knew that she was a groundbreaker who was likely to create a comedy classic. "They promised to back me for a revolutionary TV show and support my vision," Roseanne reflected.

Werner and Carsey asked fellow *Cosby* producer Matt Williams to join their team. From the start, Roseanne and Williams had many disagreements. While Roseanne wanted her on-screen family to resemble her real-life husband and children, Williams wanted his own family to serve as the model for the show.

They reached a temporary settlement: Roseanne would create the characters, and Williams would write the script. To collect ideas, Williams spent time with Roseanne and her family—who had since joined her in Los Angeles. He observed them in their daily routine at home and interviewed Roseanne for hours.

Williams developed a script from his notes. But Roseanne was disappointed with the outcome. Roseanne wanted her own name in the show's title. Williams had titled the show *Life and Stuff*. Roseanne wanted to play a character who was much like herself—outspoken and sarcastic. Instead Williams had made her character cheery and polite. Roseanne's TV sister, Jackie, was given the bolder, sassier role.

"I was going to write you as [the loud] character," Williams told Roseanne, "but I thought no one would like you."

30

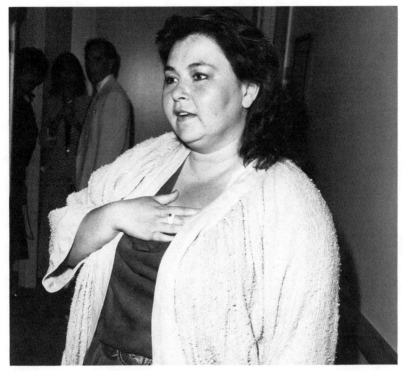
Roseanne speaks from the heart.

Roseanne was furious. "What have I done for six years?" she replied. "That's why I'm here!"

Roseanne knew her fans appreciated her just the way she was—loudmouthed. Roseanne threatened to quit the project if the script wasn't changed.

After many high-stress meetings with studio executives, Williams rewrote his script. Roseanne finally had what she wanted—the starring role in her own prime-time television sitcom: *Roseanne*.

John Goodman plays Roseanne's on-screen husband.

# 4
# Changing Channels

Bustling around the kitchen, Roseanne Conner manages her morning routine like a pro. She makes breakfast and school lunches while calmly solving crisis after crisis.

Becky's book bag is broken and she wants a new one. "You're going to use that bag until you're 30!" Roseanne tells her. D.J. begs his mother to serve him fresh-baked pie for breakfast. "It's contaminated," she jokes in reply.

The kids are squabbling and spilling cereal. To top the morning off, Darlene hands her mom a note from her history teacher. The teacher wants to meet with Roseanne later that day. Roseanne must beg her boss for time off at the factory to keep the appointment.

When Roseanne arrives at the school, her daughter's teacher has a strange complaint: Darlene has been *barking* in class.

"Well, did you tell her to stop?" Roseanne asks.

"She stopped," replies the teacher.

"So, what's the problem?"

"Your daughter barks."

"Our whole family barks," answers Roseanne. The studio audience roars with laughter. So begins the first episode of *Roseanne*, which aired on national television on October 7, 1988.

As Darlene, Sara Gilbert's razor-sharp humor rivals that of her TV mom.

Much has changed in the Conner household since the first episode was shown. Over time *Roseanne* has become a "serious comedy"—a show that examines the tough issues while still making people laugh. Viewers have watched Roseanne and Dan face a steady stream of financial problems. They have seen Dan's motorcycle business go broke and Roseanne's sister, Jackie, go into therapy.

Audiences have also witnessed the growing pains and struggles of Roseanne's teenage daughters. Becky's relationship with her boyfriend Mark brings up questions about sex, birth control, commitment, and love. Eventually, Becky elopes with Mark before graduating from high school, which comes as a devastating blow to her parents.

Darlene has also changed since the show's beginning. A witty, wisecracking child, Darlene grows up to become an even more sarcastic teenager. "You take after me," Roseanne tells her daughter in one episode.

During the show's fourth season, Darlene enters a major depression—an emotional crisis that can't be resolved in one half-hour program. Dressed from head to toe in black clothing, Darlene spends much of her time lying around on the living room couch. Roseanne isn't sure how to help her daughter, who says she just wants to be left alone.

When Roseanne asks Darlene about her troubles, she answers: "It's school. It's basketball. It's my friends.

Roseanne Conner stands up to her boss (Martin Mull) at Rodbell's Coffee Shop.

It's the way I look. It's everything." Darlene is a real teenager. Many young viewers can relate to her fears and frustrations.

From *Roseanne*'s beginning, audiences and critics agreed—the Conners were the most honest, "come-as-you-are" family in the history of television. "Barr flings truth on the table like a TV dinner," wrote one *Vogue* magazine reporter.

"The show has an unflinching commitment to tackle the hurt, tension, and joy of blue-collar America," added another critic in *TV Guide*.

*Redbook* reporter Leah Rosen observed that *Roseanne* was one of the first television shows to point out a simple fact about families: that "the very people you love most are the same people who sometimes drive you nuts."

At the end of the 1988-1989 television season, Roseanne traveled to New Jersey to star in her first feature film, *She-Devil*. Roseanne played Ruth Patchett, a plain-looking housewife whose husband falls in love with a glamorous and beautiful romance novelist.

Ruth turns the tables on her disloyal husband. She does all she can to turn his love affair to shambles. Then she changes her own life for the better, leaving her husband and opening a successful employment agency for women.

The movie was not a box-office success. But Ruth Patchett was a character Roseanne could believe in. "I wanted...some kind of soulful thing," she said after selecting the role from a number of offers, "with upheaval and truth-telling." *She-Devil* fit Roseanne's requirements.

Back in the TV studio, Roseanne worked hard on her show. The cast rehearsed all week long. Performances were taped before a live studio audience on Fridays and broadcast nationwide on Tuesday evenings. Roseanne Conner was swiftly becoming America's favorite mom. At the start of the 1989 television season, *Roseanne* jumped to the top of the Nielsen ratings.

But at home, Roseanne Barr had her own personal struggles. Her oldest daughter, 14-year-old Jessica, was admitted to a rehabilitation center for an addiction to drugs and alcohol. Roseanne called her daughter every day from the television studio. She blamed herself, in part, for Jessica's problems.

"I feel it was because I wasn't there," Roseanne explained. "Jessie needed discipline and intense structure, which we weren't providing at home."

Roseanne also faced another crisis. Her marriage to Bill Pentland had been shaky for some time. Roseanne and Bill went to see a marriage counselor and eventually decided to separate. Roseanne knew a divorce was inevitable. She also knew she was falling in love with another man.

Roseanne had met comedian Tom Arnold in 1983 at the Comedy Gallery in Minneapolis. "He killed me," remembered Roseanne. "He did weird tricks with little goldfish." One of Tom's goldfish even drove a motorcycle through a ring of fire.

Tom and Roseanne got along well and performed together a few times. The two comics had a lot in common—including a heavy build. Roseanne weighed 240 pounds, and Tom tipped the scales at 320.

Tom and Roseanne were a perfect match.

"We'd be just like best buddies," Roseanne told *Vanity Fair* magazine. "We'd always go shopping at the fat-men stores and buy the same shirts, and then we'd go onstage as twins and beat each other up."

Roseanne's life would take some surprising turns.

Roseanne and Tom kept in touch over the years, and in 1988, Roseanne hired Tom as a scriptwriter for her show. Because Roseanne was married, and because Tom and Bill Pentland were good friends, Roseanne and Tom never admitted they loved each other. "We kept pushing it back because we didn't want it to be true," Roseanne reflected.

Finally, she and Tom began to reveal their feelings for one another. They had daily phone conversations that lasted for hours. One day Roseanne asked 30-year-old Tom: "How come you've been engaged three times since I've known you and it has never worked out?"

"I've been waiting for you since I was 24," he replied.

Amidst all the changes in her personal life, Roseanne received another surprise—a phone call from the *National Enquirer*, a tabloid newspaper. A reporter claimed to have found the daughter Roseanne put up for adoption 18 years earlier.

When Roseanne gave up her baby in 1971, she left special instructions with the adoption agency: When her daughter became an adult, she could contact Roseanne if she wanted. Apparently, someone at the *Enquirer* had found the information before Roseanne's daughter, though. The newspaper planned to tell its readers—with or without Roseanne's permission—that Roseanne had been a teenage mother.

Roseanne didn't want her daughter to learn of her identity by reading a tabloid newspaper. She immediately hired a well-known Hollywood detective, Anthony Pellicano, to locate the young woman. Pellicano found her in four days.

Her name was Brandi Brown. She had grown up in Denver and had since moved to Texas with her adoptive mother. Without any hesitation, Roseanne arranged a meeting with Brandi and her mother at the Westwood Hotel in Hollywood.

With her sister Geraldine along for moral support, Roseanne arrived early at the hotel. She called the Browns' room, but Brandi and her mother were out. "Let's go have a cup of coffee," Roseanne suggested. "They'll be back soon."

As the two sisters exited the hotel, Roseanne spotted a young woman—it was Brandi! "I turned around and felt this powerful magnet," Roseanne remembers. "We looked at each other, Brandi jumped out of her seat, and we started running toward each other. We embraced and wouldn't let go of each other, hugging and crying."

Roseanne was very happy to be reunited with Brandi. They promised to visit one another as much as possible. Soon Roseanne returned to the studio to begin shooting *Roseanne's* third season. Once again, the show easily soared to the number-one position in the Nielsen ratings. Roseanne's spirits soared too.

On January 17, 1990, Roseanne and Bill Pentland were divorced. Three days later, Roseanne married Tom Arnold. Tom gave Roseanne a magnificent ring to celebrate their love. The ring had a yellow diamond in the middle with six white diamonds around the outside—one for each year of their friendship.

Roseanne and Tom made an agreement. She would take his last name if he would convert to her religion.

Tom happily converted to Judaism, and Roseanne Barr became Roseanne Arnold.

Tom agreed to help Roseanne raise her teenage children. He also took over many of the business details on the *Roseanne* set. Besides writing for the show, Tom became a manager, a producer, and even a costar—taking on the role of Dan Conner's daffy and annoying friend, Arnie.

Roseanne and Tom—with Jessica, Jake, and Jennifer—are married.

Looking good in Hollywood

Roseanne and Tom wanted more creative control over *Roseanne* and other TV projects. They asked to be named *Roseanne's* executive producers, and the Carsey-Werner Company agreed. Roseanne and Tom also decided to form their own television production company, Barnold Productions.

In the fall of 1991, Roseanne and Tom launched several ABC-TV projects, including an animated television special, *Rosey and Buddy*. The program featured the cartoon antics of child-size versions of Roseanne and Tom. *Backfield in Motion*, a made-for-TV movie, was Roseanne and Tom's first film effort. Roseanne played a divorced mom who joins her son's football team. Tom was a frustrated coach who falls in love with Roseanne. Both shows were popular with TV viewers.

Roseanne released her first compact disc in 1991, *I Enjoy Being a Girl*, with plans for a second comedy CD to follow. In her few spare moments, she worked on a new autobiography.

Roseanne was at a high point in her career. She had a happy new marriage, a top-rated sitcom, and a successful comedy career. Her future looked bright. What she didn't expect was another crisis—and a sad reminder of her past.

# 5
## *Second to None*

In October 1991, Roseanne stood before an audience of nearly 1,000 people at the Montview Boulevard Presbyterian Church in Denver. Usually when Roseanne stood on a stage, she was telling jokes. But this time, she had a serious message. "My name is Roseanne and I am an incest survivor," she told the audience.

Roseanne was the surprise guest speaker at a gathering of incest survivors, people who have been sexually molested by a family member. Trembling, Roseanne told the audience that her parents had abused her when she was a child. She explained how the memories of her abuse had been buried for many years.

Roseanne's parents denied that they abused her. But many people were pleased that someone as famous as Roseanne Arnold chose to speak publicly about a personal and painful topic.

Tom and Roseanne are slimmed down and happier than ever.

"It is very important to me that kids and other survivors know that somebody like me has gone through it too," explained Roseanne. "There is nothing harder than keeping something inside of you, than denying the truth to yourself. I felt that God wanted me to speak out."

In addition to attending a discussion group for incest survivors, Roseanne met with a therapist for support and guidance. "With treatment, you realize that it's not your fault," Roseanne remarked.

Therapy was one way for Roseanne to heal the scars from her past. She also renewed her energy and self-esteem by exercising, losing weight, and eating healthy foods. Tom joined Roseanne on a weight-loss program. Within a year, Roseanne had lost more than 50 pounds and Tom had dropped nearly 100!

Roseanne was taking good care of herself and she was proud. "I feel like the same person, only better," Roseanne exclaimed. "A lot of the negative stuff inside me is gone."

Roseanne was proud of her achievements in front of the camera too. "I really have faith in the work I do," she said. "I'm not one of those artists who thinks she's worth nothing or who suffers for her art. I'm such a [big] fan of mine it's unbelievable. I watch my stuff every day, over and over."

Roseanne signed a contract with HBO to produce several comedy projects in 1992. In June she traveled to the Guthrie Theater in Minneapolis to film a special for the cable channel. In a tribute to her roots as a stand-up comic, Roseanne—boldly costumed in a shiny gold pantsuit—performed a rowdy and hilarious routine.

When *Roseanne's* fourth season ended, the Arnolds took a short vacation and then went to work on an ABC-TV movie called *Graced Land*. The movie was shot in Ottumwa, Iowa—Tom's hometown. Many of Tom's relatives, including his two grandmothers, had small parts in the film.

In *Graced Land*, Roseanne plays Joyce Jackson, a divorced mother on welfare who is crazy about rock-and-roll star Elvis Presley. Tom plays the husband who left Joyce in 1977—on the night Elvis Presley died.

The role of Joyce Jackson appealed to Roseanne, who follows a personal rule when deciding whether or not to accept a film offer: She will only accept a part that presents women in positive ways.

"Joyce Jackson . . . is a woman who, by the standards of the normal world, has nothing to be proud of," notes *Graced Land's* author, Laura Kalpakian. "But she doesn't allow herself to be treated like a victim. Even while trying to balance the budget, she tries to find room for generosity and grace. She goes around doing good deeds in Elvis's name."

While the movie was being filmed, Roseanne and Tom made plans to build a new home in Iowa, on

1,600 acres of Ottumwa farmland. Elvis fans themselves, Roseanne and Tom decided to name their home "Our Graceland"—after Elvis Presley's estate, Graceland, in Memphis, Tennessee.

*Roseanne Barr Live from Trump Castle* was a sidesplitting HBO comedy special.

The Conner family in 1992

The 28,000 square-foot mansion is the largest house in Iowa. It has an indoor Olympic-size swimming pool and even a bowling alley! "We have dirt bikes and horses," Roseanne happily reports. "We fish, we have a boat, we have lakes. We have these real cool jalopies that we drive around."

Roseanne and Tom have many new projects in mind.

They hope to remake their favorite movie, *The Long, Long Trailer*, first produced in 1953. The original version of the film classic starred another well-known comedy duo—Roseanne and Tom's heroes—Lucille Ball and Desi Arnaz.

As the 1992-1993 television season began, Roseanne and Tom were busier than ever. Tom's own situation comedy—*The Jackie Thomas Show*—debuted in December 1992. Tom stars in the show as a former meat packer from Iowa who discovers his talent for comedy. He becomes a zany TV comedian who can't keep out of trouble. "Jackie is a combination of me and Rosie," Tom said of his TV character.

In the fall of 1992, *Roseanne* went into syndication—that is, old episodes of the show (reruns) began to appear daily on television stations across the country and around the globe. Reruns are very profitable for actors, who receive payments for rebroadcasted episodes. When her show became syndicated, Roseanne—who was already quite rich—added millions of dollars to her bank account.

While Roseanne can afford expensive houses, fancy cars, and nice clothes, she enjoys the simple things in her life the most. To relax, Roseanne likes to cook and bake. "I make turkey meat loaf and tuna fish casserole for Tom," Roseanne told *US* magazine. "Despite all this money and wealth we have, those are his two favorite meals."

Jake, Roseanne, and Tom visit Roseanne's star at the Walk of Fame.

Roseanne also likes to collect "pig things." Her California home is full of pig replicas in all sizes and colors. A tiny ceramic pig on a velvet cushion is Roseanne's favorite.

When Roseanne and Tom are working in Hollywood, they live in Brentwood, a suburb of Los Angeles. Jessica and Jennifer attend boarding school in Idaho. Jake lives at home and attends a Los Angeles-area prep school.

Roseanne, Tom, and Jake also like to spend time at their home in Iowa. In December 1992, the creative couple launched a surprising new venture—their own restaurant—"Roseanne and Tom's Big Food Diner." Roseanne and Tom built the restaurant, located in Eldon, Iowa, because every other restaurant nearby closed before dinnertime. Roseanne and Tom also plan to open a restaurant in Ottumwa.

In the near future, Roseanne and Tom would like to add a new baby to their household. "A baby is the thing Tom and I want most," says Roseanne. "As long as I have kids around, I'll be young."

Roseanne is the queen bee of comedy. Her future is full of exciting new projects and family plans. Will she stay on top? "At this point," Roseanne says, "I think I'm pretty much unbeatable."

## ACKNOWLEDGMENTS

Photographs used with permission of London Features International/Ron Wolfson: pp. 1, 2, 28, 31, 40, 44; Hollywood Book and Poster: pp. 6, 11, 34, 52; Photofest: pp. 8, 12, 23, 32, 36, 39, 46, 51, 56; Salt Lake Convention and Visitors Bureau: p. 15; East High School: p. 16; London Features International/John Roca: p. 20; Globe Photos/Ralph Dominguez: p. 24; Globe Photos/Sylvia Norris: p. 27; Globe Photos/John Barrett: p. 43; London Features International/Gregg DeGuire: pp. 48, 54. Front cover: London Features International/Ron Wolfson. Back cover: Hollywood Book and Poster.